Papoose City

by

Judy Goodspeed

Published by
Dragonfly Publishing, Inc.

PAPOOSE CITY

Non-Fiction / American History
Released in 2011

Hardback Edition
EAN 978-1-936381-29-6
ISBN 1-936381-29-X

Paperback Edition
EAN 978-1-936381-30-2
ISBN 1-936381-30-3

Published in the United States of America by
Dragonfly Publishing, Inc.
Website: www.dragonflypubs.com

Table of Contents

Dedication

This book is dedicated to the memory of my father, Buck Goodspeed, whose tales of Papoose City/Slick City prompted me to research and tell the story of the town that boomed in Hughes County, Oklahoma in 1923.

Steer roper Buck Goodspeed mounted on
"G.I." at Hobbs, New Mexico (1938)

Acknowledgements

My thanks to the following individuals: Mattie Muirhead Dillman, Mona Muirhead Campbell, Elaine Grace Keesee, Gertie Reed, Loise Chastain, P.J. Primm, Billy Bob Richardson, Pat Brinlee Ray and Oliver Brinlee, for sharing their life stories and photographs with me.

Thanks to Greg Cook for explaining the process of restoration and to Phillip Landers for sharing information about the methods of early drilling and laying pipelines.

As always, thanks to my writers group for encouragement and suggestions.

A special thanks goes to Johnnie Wingo, Naomi Tomlinson and Carol Eyster for their editing and helpful suggestions.

Many people have told stories of Papoose City, and I appreciate each bit of information. I can't name all of you, but thank you.

Without my publisher and friend, Terri Branson, I would be flapping helplessly in wind. Thank you Terri.

Introduction

DISCOVERING oil wasn't high on my priority list that May morning in 1950.

I was seven years old, out of school for the summer and anxious to escape kitchen duty so I could ride my horse, Tuffy.

When the last dish was dried, I shot out the back door and raced to the barn. Tuffy met me at the corral gate. He stood over sixteen hands and I stood about four feet, so I had to climb up on his feed trough to bridle him. I opened the gate and led Tuffy alongside it. Then I climbed to the top of the gate and mounted my horse.

I was in a hurry because Dad had a head start on me, but I was a good tracker so I would find him. Tuffy and I headed west from the barn. We crossed the creek and angled north for the canyon.

Going through the canyon was scary. It wasn't long, but it was deep, so deep that I couldn't see the top and I just knew a wolf or mountain lion waited to jump on us. When we entered the narrow passageway, I urged Tuffy into a lope. He responded, and we flew through without being attacked. I had to grip tight with my legs because there wasn't a saddle horn to hold on to. When we hit the top, Tuffy was really moving and I had to grip tighter to keep from sliding off his rump.

From the canyon we had smooth sailing to the west eighty acres where I was certain I would find Dad. I was enjoying my freedom and the lovely countryside when I noticed something different in the pasture. Riding closer I saw black liquid coming out of the ground and running into a low spot. I studied the weird stuff for a minute, and then took off.

"Tuffy, we're rich. That stuff's oil. We need to find Dad quick."

Daddy was stretching barbed wire when we found him.

I rode up yelling: "We're rich! You don't have to work anymore."

Dad grinned up at me. "You been robbing banks again?"

"No. Me and Tuffy found oil bubbling out of the ground!"

"Where?"

"Over there," I said, as I pointed.

"It's an old well site. I'll call the Corporation Commission."

The Corporation Commission sent a man out to investigate and he contacted the company responsible for the damage. The oil flowed for several days before the well was capped. Not only did we not get rich, we also had a good-sized piece of damaged land.

In my younger years I didn't think much about it as I avoided sunken well sites and pieces of cable and pipe on our property. The large concrete blocks that were derrick foundations were good to hide behind and handy for mounting your horse, but the slush pits were unsightly places to avoid. Salt scar creeks were wonderful places to hunt treasures and sail homemade boats after a rain.

As I grew older and traversed the countryside hunting quail or working cattle I became aware of the extensive damage that had been done to our land and neighboring sections. I began to pay closer attention to Dad when he told me stories. Especially stories about our land that was included in the 2,200-acre Papoose Oil field, and stories of Papoose City, also referred to as Slick City because the famous oilman Tom Slick helped develop the field. The boomtown started in 1923.

My dad, Buck Goodspeed, was seventeen years old when Slick City began. He lived on a farm two miles north and one half-mile east of where the town was located. Dad borrowed a neighbor's team of horses and a slip and went to work building sludge pits. He earned fifty cents a day. Dad worked long enough to buy a horse, and began a career in rodeo.

Sam Proctor was a friend of Dad's. They roped together and made frequent trips to Papoose City. Sam owned property near Cromwell and made thousands of dollars when the Cromwell boom began in 1923. He bought a Buick Roadster. Dad said it was the prettiest car he had ever seen and riding into town in that car caused a lot of slack-jaw.

I knew boomtowns had reputations as rough and dangerous places, so I asked Dad if they ever had any trouble. He said that most of the trouble was among the oilfield workers and gamblers and usually there was drinking involved. I had asked the question while we were riding to a neighbor's to work his cattle. We were on a county road about a mile northwest of our place when Dad reined in his horse saying: "Right here is where a young man got shot."

"Did you know him?" I asked.

"Yes. I knew him and I knew the man who shot him."

"Why did he get shot?"

"Lily, who lived up the road from here, came to the dance with an older man named Bob. Bob was married, but Lily might not have known it. He was around Papoose a lot, but he lived in Okemah. Bob was bad about going out on his wife. Anyway, he brought Lily to the dance and then he left. When it started getting late and a bit rowdy, Lily began to worry about how she was going to get home. A local young man named John offered to take her home since her house was on his way home. Lily accepted his offer.

"They hadn't been gone long when Bob came back to get her. He was furious when he couldn't find her and started asking questions. Some fool told him that she left with John.

"Sam and I found John's car on our way home. We stopped to see if he needed help and found his body in the ditch next to his car. Sam checked for a pulse but there wasn't one. We didn't move him. I stayed with the body while Sam went to Okemah for the sheriff. That was the longest night I've ever spent.

"We told the sheriff what we knew and he went to question Lily. We later found out that John had taken Lily home and was headed home himself when Bob intercepted him. Lily didn't know that Bob came back looking for her or that John had been killed. By the time the sheriff got to Okemah to question Bob, he was long gone. A few weeks later his wife and kids moved to California."

Dad never mentioned that incident again, but he did tell me about going to the mercantile and dance hall at Papoose City. He also said there were two brothels, and a movie theater.

I realize now I should have asked more questions and recorded the information while my dad was still living. Luckily, I have found several people who lived or worked in the area when Papoose City was thriving and have their stories to share.

Papoose City was located approximately twenty-three miles east of Seminole, Oklahoma, and nine miles southeast of Cromwell in Hughes and Okfuskee counties. From the intersection of Highway 9 and Highway 48, Papoose City was four miles north and three miles east. This was a sparsely populated farming community but became a booming little business center when a gusher blew in on August 25, 1923. The Papoose Drilling Company drilled the well on Joe Simon's farm and struck oil at 3,300 feet in the Cromwell sand. Black oil flowed for days.

Joe Simons was one-fourth Creek Indian, roll number 3374. In 1899 he applied for and was allotted one hundred sixty acres of

Indian land in Section 4 Township 9N Range 9E of Hughes County. In 1925 he leased blocks six and four to Slick City. After his death in 1935 the property went into probate, and Joe's wife Emma was granted the land. She lost the property in a foreclosure case in 1935.

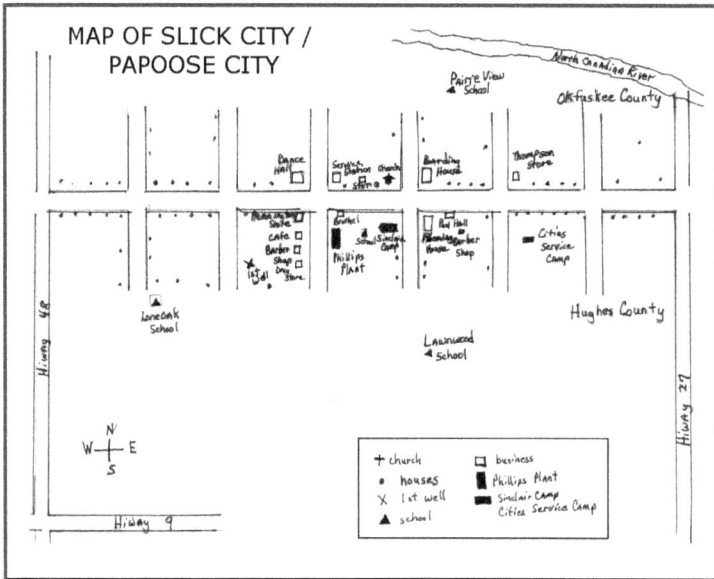

MAP OF SLICK CITY / PAPOOSE CITY

Abandoned power house located in the Sinclair camp

Present view of old well site (2011)

Concrete foundation used to support derricks

Land Damaged by saltwater (salt scars)

Unfinished capped well

Oil and water separator; oil in tank water
in wooden barrel

CHAPTER I

The Early Years

Mattie Muirhead Dillman

THIRTEEN-year-old Mattie Muirhead lived about a mile south of the Simon's Farm. It was hot and dry, typical weather for Oklahoma in August. There wasn't much activity going on as crops were laid by and the gardens yielded very little produce. Mostly, folks were yearning for relief from the heat. Little did they know that an event was about to happen that would completely change their lives.

"I was helping Mama wash the day the well blew in," Mattie recalls. "We were under a big oak tree scrubbing clothes on a rub board hoping for a little breeze when we heard a boom and a spewing noise, couldn't think what made those kinds of sounds. My brother Plaz had been visiting a neighbor and investigated what had happened. He came home to report that oil was spewing everywhere. The news excited Dad so much that he hitched up the team to the wagon and hauled and us eight kids to see the well. I don't know if I was more thrilled about the gusher or getting out of scrubbing clothes. There were people already there when we pulled up. They were just standing around looking at the oil running in a steady stream. Seemed like from that day, until I left the community years later the smell of oil-saturated dirt hung in the air."

Mattie was raised in the Lone Oak community. Her father farmed, as did most of the families in the area. The countryside was basically flat with creeks that provided water for livestock and often for the families that lived near them. Large oak, pecan, and elm trees furnished shade and firewood. There were the thorny Bois d' arc used for fence posts and honey locust whose thorns could puncture a tire. Persimmon tree sprouts were a constant problem for farmers.

The eight Muirhead children attended Lone Oak School. Typical for a farming community, school was in session when the children weren't needed at home. School was out during planting season in the spring and again in the fall when crops were harvested. One teacher taught all eight grades.

"Once that gusher came in it seemed like every time the sun came up something new had been added. Before you could blink an eye oil derricks were as common as trees. New folks began to move in to work in the oil field or to open a business.

"Tents and shotgun houses, long narrow houses that you could shoot a shotgun from the front door through the back without hitting anything, were everywhere. Our quiet community was suddenly alive with activity day and night, which, of course, we teenagers loved. We were all just poor farmers but now there were jobs. Cash money was hard to come by so farmers jumped at the chance to go to work in the oilfield. No education was needed. They were trained on the job, and as they learned they could advance to a higher position.

"My brother Sid went to work with a team of mules and a slip building slush pits. Then he became a collar pecker. A collar pecker's job was to synchronize the screwing in of a section of pipe. He stood at the collar while three men gripped the pipe with tongs. When he hit the collar, the first man in line turned the pipe with his tongs, then the second, and so on. When the third man had finished, the first was in position to begin again. So it was peck, turn, turn, turn, peck, turn, turn, turn, according to an established rhythm until the pipe was tight in the collar. It was amazing to watch because they worked fast and in perfect harmony. Sometimes one section of pipe weighed three or four hundred pounds and had to be held up with a boom. Later Sid was promoted to reading charts."

In 1924 Waite Phillips built a gasoline plant near Papoose City. When the plant which was referred to as Phillips Plant or Papoose was completed, Mattie went to work for the Clark family babysitting their two little boys. Mr. Clark was the superintendent at the Phillips Plant. The boys were no trouble. Mattie's biggest problem was cooking, but Mrs. Clark was patient and taught her how to handle kitchen duties.

After the Clark children were school age Mattie went to work for the Hyde family babysitting with their little boy. Mr. Hyde worked at Phillips Plant.

"I rode to work with Sid. I remember that Mother checked to see that Sid had a little money in his pocket before he left for work because robberies were common. The thieves would take any amount and be happy. If you didn't have any money you got a beating. We were never bothered.

"Despite the meanness and the possibility of getting robbed, Sid and I went to a neighbor's house for the dance every Saturday night. We didn't dare go to the dance hall at Papoose City. There was no law enforcement so fights, drinking, and gambling were common." Mattie smiled and her blue eyes twinkled. "I loved to dance and even though I knew Mama wouldn't approve, I danced every dance. Mother finally got wind of what I was doing. I overheard her telling Dad that she was going to have to take stern measures with me. Dad told her to leave me alone, since I came by it naturally. He loved to dance, too.

"When the beauty shop opened I could hardly wait to get a Marcel wave. With a new hairstyle I just knew I'd be the bell of the ball Saturday night. I paid my twenty-five cents and wiggled with excitement while the operator applied the hot rods to my hair. Instead of being the bell of the ball, I had to wear a hat because the beauty operator got the rods too hot and singed my hair."

Mattie went to visit a friend in Oklahoma City, and while there she met Tom Kinghorn. The couple married, and for eighteen years Mattie traveled from one oilfield to another with her husband. After Tom's death, Mattie married S.C. Dillman, a gauger for Sinclair Oil Company. The couple lived in Cromwell, Oklahoma for a few years, and then moved to Wewoka, Oklahoma.

While Mattie danced, wells were being drilled on four hundred feet spacings, or one well to every four acres. Later this was changed to one well in the center of ten acres. Crews worked day and night. The pace was so frantic it seemed they expected the oil to disappear. Once a well was started, they continued drilling nonstop until the well was completed. Mostly they hurried because of the expense involved and the desire to get money for the completed well. Also there was the danger of the walls collapsing causing the drill bit to get stuck.

There was little time for rest, much less to travel by horseback or wagon to Wetumka, which was eight or nine miles away. Realizing there was a need for supplies, food, entertainment, and lodging, businesses came to the area.

Gertie Jones Reed

SOON after oil was discovered, Pendeltons' Mercantile opened. A barbershop, beauty shop, two brothels, drug store, laundry, and dance hall joined the store. Later a boarding house, rooming house, and a church were established. These buildings were thrown together with whatever materials were handy or were pulled in by horses.

The boarding house served three meals six days a week and two meals on Sunday. The cost was twenty-five cents per meal. Sack lunches could be purchased after lunch on Sunday for those who needed an evening meal. The boarding house quickly became a popular place and an extra girl was needed to wait tables.

At that time fifteen-year-old Gertie Jones lived with her father and four siblings on a farm approximately six miles from Papoose City. The road they lived near is now Highway 27.

Gertie's mother died of a cerebral hemorrhage, in 1917, when Gertie was nine years old. When Cassey, the oldest girl, married and left home, Gertie became the cook, babysitter, and housekeeper for the family. She was fifteen when her life drastically changed. Roy Reed came to visit his brother and sister-in-law who lived next door to the Jones family.

"I'll never forget that day," Gertie said. "Dad had brought home a wagon load of peaches for me to can. After putting up peaches all-day I decided to rest for awhile. It was hot, so I stripped off my dress, down to the muslin slip that I wore under it, and went to sit under the oak tree. That's when a strange man drove up. He walked over, tipped his hat, and said, 'Hi, I'm Roy Reed. I came by to see my brother and noticed you, thought it would be neighborly to say hello.' I couldn't run or hide, so I smiled, told him my name, and visited with him for a little while. Lord, I was embarrassed, but also quite smitten."

Roy began to visit his brother often and always dropped by to say hello to Gertie. Then he began coming for dinner and most every Sunday afternoon. Things were going well for the young couple until the Jones' home burned, and Mr. Jones transferred to Wewoka, Oklahoma. Gertie and Roy were twenty miles apart.

"There were no paved roads, and it was a wet fall. The roads were so muddy that Roy couldn't drive to see me," Gertie said. "Finally, we had a dry spell and Roy came with news that they needed help at the boarding house in Papoose City. Getting the job would mean I'd be closer to Roy. I asked Dad about going to work, but he wouldn't hear of it. Roy and I cooked up a plan.

"As soon as Dad left for work the next morning I packed my extra dress and started walking to Holdenville."

A kind gentleman offered Gertie a ride so she accepted. After she was in the truck, she realized the man worked with her father. She just knew that he would tell her dad and he would come after her. The gentleman let her off on Main Street.

"From Holdenville I caught the train to Wetumka. Roy met me at the train station and took me to Papoose City to apply for the job. I was hired on the spot.

"My day began at four cutting up grapefruit for breakfast at six. Breakfast consisted of grapefruit, bacon, eggs, biscuits, gravy, jelly and coffee. There were two long tables that seated about thirty each. When we started serving, I was responsible for one table, and Juanita Hughes took care of the other. We had to keep the bowls full. The men were always polite and good to help us by holding up empty bowls and stacking their dirty dishes. As soon as one man finished eating, we cleared his place so someone else could sit down and eat.

"When breakfast was finished I started peeling potatoes for lunch. We had one main course, usually meatloaf, fried chicken, chicken and dumplings, or stew. There were a variety of vegetables, plus potatoes and cornbread. After lunch was finished, I started peeling potatoes for supper. Supper was stew or soup and, you guessed it, lots of potatoes and cornbread.

"I spent most of the day peeling potatoes, but it was a good job. I shared a room with one of the cooks, even had my own drawer to put my extra clothes in. My salary was five dollars a week. That was a lot of money in 1923.

"There was a hand pump in the kitchen, so we didn't have to carry water. Besides Juanita and me, there were two cooks and a man to wash dishes and run errands. Light was provided by gas instead of kerosene. Compared to the year after my mother died, this was easy."

Gertie paused for a moment, as if uncertain about sharing that difficult time with me. Then she began. "I was nine and my older sister Cassey was eleven when Mama died. We were living on a farm in Tucumcari, New Mexico at the time. There were four younger children. The baby was only six months old. Dad was sharecropping on two farms a ways from where we lived and could only make it home Saturday after work. He would bring supplies and check on us, then return to work on Sunday evening. We couldn't leave for Oklahoma because Dad had to lay the crops by. By the time he had the crops in, it was close to winter and the weather wasn't fit for traveling across the country in a wagon. Dad decided to continue to work so that meant we kids were left alone.

"Cassey was responsible for milking, feeding the livestock and other outside chores. I did the cooking and took care of the baby. We alternated days going to school because the younger kids couldn't be left alone.

"When the weather started getting cold Dad moved the cook stove and beds into the cellar. He was afraid we would freeze in the house. Miraculously, we all survived. As soon as the weather allowed, we moved to Oklahoma where Dad had relatives."

Sunday afternoon was the only free time Gertie had and the only time Roy could visit. Once or twice she worked Sunday by herself and gave Juanita the day off. The next Sunday Juanita worked for Gertie. That was the time she met Roy's parents.

"I got lonesome to see my dad and brothers and sisters so Roy took me to visit one Sunday afternoon," Gertie said. "Dad was courting a woman and was much more concerned about getting his shirt ironed than visiting. I ironed his shirt and off he went to see his girl. He had forgiven me for running off and didn't object to me and Roy getting married."

The boarding house closed in January, 1925. Gertie lived with Roy's parents until she and Roy married on June 2, 1925. During her years at the boarding house Gertie only left a few times. She went to Wetumka to buy a pair of shoes, to visit Roy's family who lived about a mile north of the boarding house and to visit her family in Wewoka.

Roy farmed for a few years then went to work for Phillips Oil Company. When the company wanted him to transfer to Wewoka he quit and went back to farming. He and Gertie had four children. After Roy's death, Gertie remarried and again outlived her husband. Gertie passed away in 2007 at the age of one hundred years and a few months.

Ethel Jordan Grace

ETHEL Jordan Grace was born in 1924, the second daughter of Lester and Rena Jordan. While she was still an infant, her father moved his family from Okmulgee County near Morris, Oklahoma, to Hughes County near Wetumka, Oklahoma. The move was in conjunction with an oil boom in which Mr. Jordan's boss, T.B. Slick, held a considerable interest.

Mrs. Jordan wasn't happy when they arrived at the new job and found there were no houses to rent. The family lived in a tent. The uneven ground made it difficult to find a spot to set the baby's highchair. Ethel toppled over a few times and once suffered a cut on her nose. Several other families also lived in tents and one family even lived in a piano crate. In time houses were built by the oil company for its employees.

T.B. Slick sold Slick Oil Company to Sinclair Prairie Oil Company and left Hughes County. He asked Mr. Jordan to go with him, but he declined. He liked Hughes County and knew that he could go to work for Sinclair Prairie.

In a short amount of time there were three oil camps within a two-mile radius. Houses lined the county line road and the camp houses were provided for workers. Phillips built a large plant. There were about twenty houses at Phillips Plant and also a school. Ethel and her family lived in the Sinclair camp area, which was about a mile east of Phillips Plant.

There were now three Jordan sisters; Alice, Ethel, Darlene and a cousin Leona who came to live with them when her mother died. The girls attended Lawnwood School. They walked across country three-quarters of a mile rather than going the long route by road. On Sunday they walked to Phillips Plant to attend Sunday school that was held in the schoolhouse.

One of Ethel's fondest memories was playing basketball. There were no gyms at that time so all games were played outside on a dirt court. All of the Jordan girls played basketball at Lawnwood and continued playing throughout their high school years at Bearden.

Ethel graduated in May of 1941. She married Lois Levi (Turk) Grace in June of the same year. Her oldest sister, Alice had married Turk's brother Harold three years earlier. The brothers worked together in the oil field and lived near each other. Turk and Ethel had two children: Elaine, born April 22, 1942, and Irwin, born April 5, 1944. Harold and Alice had six children: Leota, Virginia, Billy, Bobby, Helen, and Stephen. The cousins were so close that they thought of each other as brothers and sisters.

After Turk and Ethel married, they lived with Ethel's parents in a little house southwest of the Sinclair Oil Camp. When the elderly couple moved to Texas, Turk and Ethel continued to live in their house. Several years later they moved to a small house southeast of the Sinclair Camp and Turk worked as a gauger and pumper for Louie V. Kahn. Their final move as a couple was to a house located at the site of the Sinclair Camp.

The Grace family was very active in church activities. Turk studied and became an ordained minister and preached for many years. Every Sunday as they traveled to church they picked up neighbors along the way. They also were active in all of their children's school functions. Elaine and Irwin attended Lawnwood School until it closed in 1953 when the enrollment dropped to six students. The Grace children began school at Wetumka and both graduated from there. Irwin played football, both he and Elaine played basketball.

Ethel never worked outside the home other than serving on the election board. She enjoyed gardening, reading, and working crossword puzzles. She lived in Hughes County on the same section of land for sixty-five years. When the Tulsa World began rural delivery, Ethel subscribed. She worked the crossword puzzle everyday from 1960 until her death in 2006. Turk's hobbies included raising cattle, quail hunting, and being the local barber.

It was a sad day in the community when Turk Grace died of a heart attack at sixty-nine years of age. He and Ethel had been married forty-eight years. Although still capable of living in the country Ethel chose to move to Okemah. When her health began to fail, she moved to Henryetta to be near her daughter. She lived in Henryetta for twelve years and spent her final days in a nursing home in Okemah.

Gusher coming in

Elmer Yockum and Mattie Muirhead ready for the dance

Papoose City / Slick City main street in 1923

Mattie Muirhead Dillman on her 96th birthday in 2006

Phillips workers digging a ditch in the Papoose Oil Field

Foreman Sid Muirhead supervises workers preparing
the ditch for pipe

Taking a break to shoot a game of craps

Collar pecker tapping a tune as workers screw
together sections of pipe

Gertie Jones in front of Reed home in 1925

Juanita Hughes and Gertie Jones taking a break

Gertie Jones in front of the boarding house where she
worked at Papoose City; she was married in that dress

Jordan sisters: Alice (left), Darlene (in front),
and Ethel (right)

Bearden basketball team; back row second from left
is Ethel Jordan with her sister Alice on her left

Ethel Jordan Grace, husband Lois (Turk) Grace,
with children Irwin and Elaine

CHAPTER II

Camp Life

Loise McCasland Chastain

PEAK production of the Papoose field was in 1925 when ninety completed wells were producing 39,814 barrels of oil per day. Although the field steadily declined and drilling stopped, Phillips Plant continued operation, and twelve families lived in the Phillips camp. Five families lived in the Sinclair Camp and five families lived in the Cities Service Camp. Each oil camp owned producing wells and provided housing for their employees.

Loise McCasland Chastain was raised in the Slick Oil Camp, which was owned by Tom Slick and was located about one half-mile east of the Phillips Plant. Tom Slick sold Slick Oil Company to the Prairie Oil Company, who in turn sold to Sinclair Oil Company. Her father moved the family to the camp in 1923 and began working as a roustabout.

By 1925 the fast paced drilling had stopped and workers left as rapidly as they had come. When the crews left so did much of the income for the town, which soon faded away as was the case for Papoose City. Now most of the population consisted of families living in the oil camps and local farmers. There was such a large number of children in the camps that Lawnwood School was overflowing so although Phillips had built a school near the plant, later a second school was built about one and a half miles east of the plant. The McCasland children walked about a mile from the Sinclair Camp to Lawnwood School.

The McCaslands were furnished a house which consisted of a living room, dining room, two bedrooms, and a kitchen. There was no running water or electricity. Drinking and cooking water came from a well and was pumped by hand. Bathing and wash water were furnished from a large wooden storage tank located near the camp. Lights and the refrigerator were powered by natural gas.

Russ Godard was superintendent of the Sinclair Camp and had the only house with an indoor bathroom. When Mr. Godard transferred to Seminole, Mr. McCasland became superintendent and moved his family into the big house.

There were five families in the camp and a total of nineteen children, nine of which were McCaslands. Camp life offered many opportunities for the kids. "I learned to swim in the water storage tank," Loise said. "We climbed to the top of the water tank, and the boys stretched a rope across the top. Then Whitey got on one side, and Alan pitched me into the water. I dog paddled across and didn't have to grab the rope once.

"Other favorite activities were riding the rods in the powerhouse, climbing derricks, and walking the pipelines across the creeks. Of course all of these things were forbidden, but we did them anyway.

"Tennis was popular at the time, so we camp kids decided we needed a tennis court. Pat Scott, a local farmer, gave us enough land to make a court, and we went to work. We cleared the area of rocks and weeds then Dad sprayed it with gasoline to kill the grass. After it was smoothed and leveled, we marked our boundary lines with a hoe. Now all we needed were rackets and a net.

"I chopped cotton one summer to buy a tennis racket. The racket cost $3.50 and was one of six in the camp.

"We were sewing burlap sacks together for a net when our parents decided we were serious and chipped in to buy a net for us. We shared rackets with those who didn't have one, and we usually played doubles so more could play. Lefty Vaughan and I won the mixed doubles championship at the Wetumka Invitational Tournament. Tennis was one of my favorite activities for many years.

"Most of the kids from the camps attended Lawnwood School, which was a little over a mile south of the camp. There was quite a gang when we started to school every morning, and the gang grew as we went along. After graduating from the eighth grade, students could go to high school at Wetumka or Bearden."

Loise graduated from Bearden High School in 1941. She went to Wetumka and found a job at Neal's Drugstore.

"My job was to take care of the store while Mr. Neal filled prescriptions. I was the soda jerk and clerk. My pay was $5.00 a week. I actually took home $4.87. Out of that $4.87, I paid $1.00 a week for a bedroom, sitting room, and kitchen that belonged to Ma and Pa Swain. I had a weekly beauty shop appointment for twenty-five cents a visit. Most of the time I took my lunch to work, but occasionally I treated myself to a bowl of red top stew at Verna and Mac McGibney's Café. Verna was famous for her red top stew, which was stew with chili on top. It was delicious. Entertainment was pretty cheap. It cost fifteen cents to go to the movie at the Redskin Theater. Pop and popcorn were a nickel each," Loise said.

Loise met Manuel Chastain when he came into the drug store. They married in 1945 and lived in California for a while then they moved to various places following oil field work.

The Chastains moved back to Wetumka in 1972 and Manuel worked as a pumper. He was injured on the job and retired to raise cattle and horses.

In 1998 Manuel and Loise moved to Charleston, Arkansas to be near their oldest daughter. Loise still lives in Charleston.

"I have wonderful memories of the Sinclair Camp. Many of the friends I made in camp are still friends today. It was a sad day in 1944 when Dad was transferred to Texas."

Billy Bob Richardson

BILLY Bob smiles as he recalls, "It was always an exciting time when Uncle Frank Phillips came to visit. Someone would meet us at the bus stop and tell us to go to the community building. We knew then that we were going to town. Uncle Frank met us at the building and we all loaded up in the back of a big truck. Our first stop was at the Hamburger Inn for a hamburger and a Double Cola. When we finished eating, we rode to downtown Seminole and parked in the middle of Main Street. We went to J.C. Penney's or C.R. Anthony's for shoes, a bundle of socks, overalls for the boys and dresses for the girls. Uncle Frank was kind and generous and we all loved him. As I grew older, I realized that Frank Phillips was not only Dad's boss, he also owned one of the largest oil companies in Oklahoma."

Billy Bob was the fifth of eight children born to John and Elma Richardson. John Richardson first worked as a pumper for Phillips Oil Company, was promoted to foreman, and later to superintendent. One of the jobs as superintendent was overseeing the construction of gasoline plants. One of those plants was located at Papoose in Hughes County.

"We moved a lot so I don't remember too much about the early years. I do know that all oil camps were pretty much the same. Small frame houses, large wooden tanks, one to store drinking water and another in case of a fire. We swam in the fire tank but knew better to get caught in the drinking water. All around the area were stacks of pipe and discarded equipment. These were wonderful places to play hide and seek or tag. One time Margaret Parkhurst and I decided to hide in an abandoned heater treater. We crawled through the open door and hid in the dark recesses of the large treater. Someone closed the door. We were locked in and there was no way out. At first we panicked then settled down for a long wait, thinking that someone would miss us at the supper table. Sure enough Bobby Green came to our rescue.

"There was always something to do and someone to play with in an oil camp. When the Richardsons lived on the Dixie Lease near Wewoka, there were so many kids that the school bus had to make two trips. The bus was small with three bench seats, one on each side and one down the middle.

"At the bus stop there was a cattle guard. When we got off the bus one afternoon one of the kids threw a ball and it went between the pipes of the guard and landed in the hole underneath. My brother Harold tried to retrieve the ball but couldn't quite reach it so he stuck his head and shoulder between the pipes. He got the ball but couldn't pull his head back between the pipes. We had to go get help. One of the welders came and cut the pipe to get Harold out.

"Another activity we enjoyed was riding the wide belt about forty feet long that ran from the engine to a walking beam. The beam turned the jack that pumped the oil out of the well. It was dangerous but not one kid got hurt."

The family never had much money, certainly not enough to pay admission to a football game. "We discovered the oil derricks next to football field, so we climbed up and watched the game. It was great fun and probably the best seat in the house."

When the family moved to Seminole, Billy Bob got his first job washing dishes at the Hamburger Inn. From Seminole the family moved to Okemah. Billy Bob recalls visiting Clark's Barber Shop. The shoeshine chair wasn't being used so I asked if I could shine shoes.

"Mr. Clark thought that was a good idea, so I polished shoes after school for twenty-five cents a pair. On the weekend I popped popcorn and cleaned the Crystal Theater."

From Okemah the family moved to Snomac, a small community near Seminole. Billy Bob was in the third grade. The school at Snomac consisted of two rooms for grades one through eight. At Christmas the students presented a program for the community. Every student had a speaking part except Billy Bob, he was the official curtain puller. "I was a little put out that I didn't get to speak so when the teacher introduced me I stepped from behind the curtain saying, 'I'm glad to know everyone of you.' That incident drew a chuckle or two from the audience."

The next move was to Shawnee. Billy Bob remembers that they had been there about six months when the U. S. entered World War II. It was also about this time that his parents separated. "Mom just got fed up with Dad working all the time. Dad came to see us every weekend. They finally went back together and we moved back to Seminole."

Many changes occurred because of the war. Items such as sugar, gasoline, and rubber were rationed. Times were hard. Batteries were difficult to get and they were in great demand in the oil field. Luther Ledbetter, owned a battery shop in Wewoka. He taught Billy Bob how to rebuild discarded batteries. Mr. Cullum, the shop foreman for Phillips at Seminole, gave Billy Bob a bunch of batteries to rebuild.

Billy Bob constructed a steamer that consisted of a bucket with a pipe wielded in the center. Water was poured into the bucket and heated. Steam came up the pipe. A hose connected to the pipe allowed Billy Bob to direct the hot steam onto a battery so that the cells could be separated. In between each cell was a piece of cardboard that kept the cells from touching each other. When they were free from the cardboard individual cells could be examined. A bad cell had a hole in the plate and could not be repaired. The bad cells were replaced with good cells from another battery. Once the cells and cardboard were in place, they were sealed with tar and placed on the charger. Business boomed when news spread that batteries were available. Phillips started sending batteries from Oklahoma City for Billy Bob to rebuild. He made eight dollars a battery. When the war ended, so did Billy Bob's job.

More or less at loose ends after graduating from Wewoka High School in 1947, Billy Bob joined the Air Force. He attended Officers Candidate School and did his flight training at Kelly Air Force Base in San Antonio, TX. During the Korean War, he was stationed on

Guam flying C47 and P51 fighter planes and sometimes C54 cargo planes. Billy Bob flew twenty-seven successful missions without suffering any injuries.

He was soldier of the month while stationed in Guam and was awarded the Airman's Metal for pulling a pilot from a burning P51 that crashed at the end of the runway in Kearney, Nebraska.

He returned home with thoughts of re-enlisting but went to work in the oilfield to make some money before making a final decision. Billy Bob worked for Sid Hazelrigg, who owned a trucking company, making eight dollars an hour. On the morning of July 19, 1952, Sid asked Billy Bob to drive a truck loaded with seven quarts of nitroglycerin and two cases of dynamite to a well site near Asher, Oklahoma.

"That truck don't have any brakes," Billy Bob told Sid.

"Just use the emergency brake. I really need that stuff delivered," Sid said.

Billy Bob headed for Asher with the load of explosives. All went well until he reached the South Canadian River Bridge. When he topped the one lane-bridge and started down the other side there was a car stalled on the end of the bridge. He pulled the emergency brake with no results. Desperate to keep from killing anyone in the car he tried to slow the truck by rubbing against the railing. The friction ignited the dynamite and the truck exploded. A piece of pipe tore through Billy Bob's side. Parts of the grill ripped away one side of his face and lodged in his mouth.

"I was in critical condition for six months. Doctor Padberg in Ada saved my life. After I was stable enough to be moved, he sent me to Saint Anthony's Hospital in Oklahoma City where Doctor Sampbell began plastic surgery. It took many years to complete the surgeries to reconstruct my face."

In time Billy Bob healed enough to become tired of the hospital. One afternoon he asked to go roller-skating. His doctor said that he could go, but to be in early as he was to have surgery the next morning. Billy walked to the skating rink.

He enjoyed the activity and when he noticed a young lady sitting alone, he asked her to be his partner for the couples' skate. They enjoyed skating together then went their separate ways.

Billy Bob began walking back to the hospital. He became alarmed when he heard footsteps behind him so he stopped to see if he was being followed. It was the girl from the skating rink. She lived near the hospital and was on her way home. They sat and visited. Her name was Norma Behrens, and she was from Russet, Oklahoma. Her father worked as a sharecropper for Fred Chapman. She was the oldest of twelve children. Mr. Chapman thought so much of Norma that he sent her to Draughns' Business School.

Norma was sitting by his bed when he awoke from surgery. She visited him often. When he was well enough they went skating again. The couple became serious and Norma invited Billy Bob to spend Christmas with her family. He wanted to go but didn't think it would look good if they weren't married. Although they had only known each other six weeks, he asked Norma to marry him. She said yes.

"I had ten dollars to my name. I went to B.C. Clark's jewelry and told Mr. Clark my situation. He agreed to take my money and let me have a ring and I was to pay him the balance when I could. My dad loaned me five dollars for a marriage license. A friend gave me ten dollars to pay the preacher, and my brother-in law gave me fifty dollars. We sure didn't start out with much."

The newlyweds moved behind Bethel School near Holdenville. They planned to a make a living raising chickens. "We raised two bunches of chickens. The first bunch did okay, but from the second bunch we lost four thousand to coccidiosis. Our great plans weren't working out too well."

It was while living near Holdenville that the hot water heater in their home exploded. The couples' infant son, Billy Bob Jr. was badly burned and later died from his injuries.

"I'd had enough with chicken farming, so Norma and I bought a restaurant in Chickasha, Oklahoma. That wasn't a good move. We didn't do well in the restaurant business so I got a job with Haliburton. We went to Brownfield, Texas where I worked as a pipe cementer. From Brownfield I was sent to Snyder, Texas. The company paid all of our moving expenses, but I didn't have enough money for food. First and only time I had to ask my mother to help me out. She wired me twenty dollars."

Billy Bob decided to go to electronics school at Okmulgee, Oklahoma. The family lived in Preston, Oklahoma, which is a small town near Okmulgee. Bobby was born there in 1954. When he was a year old he was stricken with polio. His leg became infected with ostiomyilitis (infection of the bone marrow). A friend approached Billy Bob and Norma about taking Bobby to St. Louis, Missouri to the Shriner Hospital. Billy Bob was reluctant, but finally agreed.

"We went by train to St. Louis. The staff and doctors at the hospital were wonderful. It was hard to leave our little boy, but we felt that he was in good hands. He remained in the hospital for about a year. Norma and I visited when we could. They saved Bobby's leg. He returned home a healthy boy."

Bobby graduated from Oklahoma State University with a teaching degree, but only taught for a short time. He began a construction company in Oklahoma City and in 2011 was elected to Imperial Potentate of the Oklahoma Shriners.

The Richardsons' liked the community and decided to settle there so Billy Bob paid two hundred fifty dollars for a lot. When the number of children reached five Billy Bob told Norma, "We need a bigger house. I borrowed money against the lot and bought building materials. Norma, the kids and I started to work. Everyday the boys got off the school bus at the building site, and our daughter Patsy went home to cook supper. We worked hard and built a nice house. A guy came along and wanted to buy the house. I told him that it was for my family and besides I wouldn't sell the lot. He came the next day and upped the offer and said that he would move the house to another location. When he made a third offer, I sold him the house. We built another one and it also sold. When the number reached four, I told Norma told that we should go into the house building business. So we gave the lot to the school, moved to Bristow, Oklahoma, and started building roll-off houses."

While at Bristow Billy Bob went to work for Spartan Aircraft which was owned by J. Paul Getty. His job was to build mobile homes. These small trailers were top of the line and in great demand. Billy Bob delivered Spartan trailers to many places, but one that intrigued him was Newport Beach, California. Bob Hope and Bing Crosby built a private golf course at Newport Beach and wanted a number of the Spartan trailers to house their guests. This was a private club and very ritzy.

"This was quite a place and I got to know Bob and Bing pretty well."

Just before Spartan stopped making mobile homes J. Paul Getty had an elaborate house build for King Saud, the ruler of Saudi Arabia. The carpet had real gold thread throughout, and there was a small throne. A special trailer was built to transport the house to Houston and from there it went by ship to Saudi Arabia. The gift got J. Paul Getty started in the Saudi oil business.

Norma and Billy Bob decided to find a nice place and take it easy.

"We were flying around near Coleman, Oklahoma and spotted an acreage for sale. I landed the plane on the highway and inquired about the land. We settled the deal that day and later build a nice home there."

All of their children graduated from Coleman High School. Bobby, Johnny, Mike, and Terry graduated from Oklahoma State University and Patsy graduated from East Central University.

With the kids all in college Billy Bob and Norma moved to a cabin on Lake Texoma. Billy Bob built houses in Oklahoma and Texas. The housing business wasn't doing well so one of his hands suggested that they try building stock and horse trailers. Business boomed.

"I was running myself to death hauling materials and trying to stay ahead of the demand. When the owner of W&W Trailers approached me about selling, I sold out."

Norma's father became ill so they moved to Mannsville, Oklahoma to help care for him. Billy Bob built houses in Ardmore. It was while at Mannsville that Norma was diagnosed with cancer. She died in 1983. Billy Bob was lost. When his former Air Force commander offered him a job flying a mail route he eagerly accepted. The company, IBC Pacific, was based in the Philippines. Billy Bob began flying mail from Manila to Japan, Hong Kong, Russia, India, or wherever else it needed to go.

"The mail was sorted into four-foot by five-foot aluminum containers with labels on the outside stating their destinations. Once the containers were loaded onto the plane I would fly to each destination, pick up mail coming back to the U.S. and fly back. Around Christmas we would often fly the long 747 to Japan and pick up new Toyota cars to bring to the U.S. for Christmas presents. I could haul seven cars in the big 747. We had a short 747 that would haul twelve passengers, the mail and a flight attendant."

In 1992, Billy Bob met a flight attendant from the Philippines. They became friends. She was divorced and had two daughters. When Billy Bob was in town they often went to a movie or to the Jolly Bee, which is similar to McDonald's, to eat. The couple married and moved to Shawnee, Oklahoma where Billy Bob is again in the construction business.

"People that lived in the oil camps were often looked down upon and called oilfield trash. I wouldn't trade one minute of my life spent in those camps. I learned to work hard and to face challenges. Many of the kids I grew up with went on to become very successful."

Oilmen left to right: Waite Phillips, (unknown), (unknown), Tom Slick, Frank Phillips, J. Paul Getty

Clockwise from top left: Lorene, Jewell, Arnold, Loise,
Allen, and Whitie McCasland

A. F. (Berry) McCasland Family

Wooden derrick in Papoose Field

Billy Bob Richardson at home in Shawnee, Oklahoma

CHAPTER III

The Final Days

P. J. Primm

IN 1945 P.J. Primm's father, Paul, was transferred from the Mid-Continent Gas Plant in Cromwell, Oklahoma to Phillips Plant when Mid-Continent bought the plant and Papoose oil and gas field. This was a move of approximately eight miles. All of the plant employees were leaving, so just Mr. Primm, his wife Gwen, and seven-year old son P.J. occupied the once thriving camp. There remained the superintendent's house, which would be occupied by the Primm family. The eighteen houses that had housed the now transferred employees were sold to the occupants for one dollar each. The houses were then cut in half and hauled away on trucks. Each two houses shared a double garage; these too were hauled away.

Finally, all that was left was the house that P.J. and his parents occupied. P.J. recalls: "The house consisted of a living room, kitchen, bathroom, two bedrooms, and a large front porch. Next to the house there was a nice garage for our 1936, two door sedan, Model A Ford. Dad later enclosed the porch so that Mother could have a washing machine. The water from the well was red for a minute when it came out of the faucet and tasted awful. Mother had to let it run a bit before started the laundry or everything would be pink. I didn't like the water, but I loved to climb the water tower. I could see for miles and pretended to be the lookout for the whole community. However, climbing the water tower was an activity saved for the afternoons my parents took a nap."

Moving meant changing schools. Mrs. Primm enrolled P.J. in the elementary school in Wetumka for the fall term. She didn't inquire about the bus route just assumed that P.J. would be picked up the first day of school. P.J. waited and waited until his parents took him to school and questioned why he wasn't picked up. They were informed that the bus only went as far as Thompson's Store. P.J.

would have to walk two miles in order to have a ride to school.

Each week day morning P.J. would leave home an hour before time to catch the bus. It was a long walk for a seven-year old and sometimes hazardous because of the children, dogs, and a red rooster that occupied a residence along his route.

"I tiptoed by the house each morning but one of the thousand dogs would spot me and run out barking, then the other dogs would join him. The kids ran out, and there were several of them, to tease me and throw rocks at me. Even the red rooster added to my misery by trying to spur me. Dad ended my trauma by driving me to Thompson's store. On muddy or cold days he even picked up the rascals who had terrorized me."

Mrs. Primm made many trips to school and to the county superintendent's office, but all to no avail. She was about to give up when someone suggested that she take P.J. for a physical. If there was anything wrong with him, the bus would have to come to get him. Mr. and Mrs. Primm took him to the doctor in Holdenville that the county schools used. The doctor discovered that P.J. couldn't see out of his left eye. He wrote a letter to the superintendent of Wetumka Schools stating that P.J. should not walk two miles to the bus stop. The letter was ignored. Mrs. Primm confronted the superintendent and finally P.J.'s ride arrived.

"The bus driver wasn't happy about having to drive the extra miles and he let me know about it the first day. For the next eight years he and I had problems. He never even thanked my dad for driving when the roads were too bad for the bus to make its route. Our old Model A was the only vehicle that could handle the mud, and sometimes if the water was over the road, even Dad couldn't get through."

When not in school, P.J. lived in a wonderland that other kids could only dream about and even though an only child he said he was never lonely.

"There was a laboratory that contained all kinds of chemicals and even Bunsen burners. I mixed chemicals and made all sorts of concoctions, but most of my experiments involved mercury. Mercury was fun. Phillips' workers simply walked away without changing anything, leaving a wonderful playroom for a little boy.

"One night about two years after we moved there the lab caught fire and burned to the ground. It looked like a fireworks show, with pieces of tin flying off the gas lines and chemicals exploding. Dad thought lightning struck the lab, but I think an animal got in and knocked something over."

In addition to the laboratory there was over a mile of sidewalk and four concrete tennis courts, perfect places for the roller skates that clipped onto your shoes. P.J. honed his racing skills on the straight sidewalks and perfected his circles on the tennis courts. When he tired of skating, he could rest in the shade of the huge smokestacks or fish in the cooling pond that his dad stocked with bass, perch and catfish. The fish along with bullfrog legs caught at the pond graced the Primms' table many evenings.

There were three large cellars in the area. Mr. and Mrs. Primm wouldn't go inside them but P.J. did. With his grandfather's help he made the cellar closest to the house his secret cave. His hideaway was cozy with a cot, short-wave radio, candles, some old furniture, and a couple of lanterns.

Over the years the family witnessed several tornado funnels. One actually passed a few hundred yards from the house.

"I watched the funnel and just knew that it had destroyed our neighbor Alvie Ferguson's house. I raced out the next morning expecting to see a vacant spot where the house had been, but the tornado had cut a swatch between his place and the plant. Even after that close call Mom and Dad wouldn't go to the cellar," P.J. recalled.

There was usually some kind of activity going on around the field, but P.J. was surprised when a crew of welders began to disassemble the thirty-five thousand-barrel oil tanks that were across the road from the plant. The men worked for weeks using cutting torches to the take the tanks apart. Mr. Primm explained that oil production had dropped so much that the oil tanks were no longer needed. The oil produced was hauled out in trucks to the refinery in Tulsa. When P.J. went to inspect the now vacant area he found thousands, perhaps millions, of rivets scattered on the ground.

The Saturday morning after the men left his dad said, "Come with me," and headed across the road.

"I followed wondering where we were going and why Dad had two five-gallon buckets. When he began picking up rivets and putting them in a bucket, I got the picture. For the next seven years I filled two or three buckets a week. When I had picked up all that were visible Dad handed me a rake and I uncovered many more rivets. On Saturday, we hauled the filled buckets to Wetumka and Dad sold the rivets at Ed Hick's junkyard. The money was taken to the bank and put into a savings account for my college education. I wish that I had kept track of how many buckets I filled. I know it was a bunch."

P.J. didn't hang around the engine room much. The big engines made a lot of noise and were frightening. When Mr. Primm took over the plant sixteen large Bessemer engines weighing approximately 31,738 pounds each pumped gas from the plant via pipelines to Bartlesville, Oklahoma. Later when gas production at Phillips Plant slowed down gas production at Cromwell, Oklahoma was still good. A pipeline was laid from Phillips Plant to Highway 48 where it joined the Cromwell line. This even more reduced production at Phillips Plant and the need for so many engines. All but four Bessemers were shut down.

"I was fascinated with the laying of the pipeline. The men didn't mind, so I tagged along while they used shovels to dig three or four miles of ditch. Next, they strung out the pipe, then welded the joints of pipe together. Watching such hard labor made me work more on my college fund," P.J. said.

There were still several gas wells pumping and sometimes in cold weather, the gas pressure would get low and a well would shut down. When that happened, the big engines also shut down.

"Dad seemed to have a sixth sense where those engines were concerned. If an engine went down in the middle of the night, he was up and gone to find the problem. Many times I remember him coming home early in the morning covered in oil and dirt. After he got the gas well running, he had to get the Bessemer going again which meant turning the flywheel that weighted about 3,000 pounds and had a 78-inch diameter. I don't know how he managed by himself but he always did."

There were other families, most of them farmers, who lived in the area and visited with the Primms. One family named McDaniel, had lived in the community before the Primms arrived, moved away and then returned. The McDaniels and Primms became good friends.

"Mr. McDaniel told me stories about Papoose City. He said that it was once a town with stores, cafes and churches, and a place where women entertained the men who worked in the oil field. He married the daughter of the woman in charge of the women who came to Papoose City. I thought that maybe these women came to play cards or something. Took me a while to figure it out.

"Mr. McDaniel explained that the plant helped many survive the depression and that when World War II started men left for the service and the oil field began to lose production."

A common practice during the early oil production years was using distillate or drip gas that was produced along with the oil. This was a waste product but many people would blow the drip from the line and use it in their cars and farm machinery. Teenagers loved the free gas and sought the wells that produced the most drip.

When a new boss took over at Cromwell, he told Mr. Primm that the farmers were not to continue getting drip gas. There was no reason given but he was adamant about stopping the practice. Mr. Primm told the locals that they could no longer have the drip. One farmer who had been his friend never spoke to him again.

In 1955 the plant was sold and Paul Primm was transferred from Phillips Plant to Goliad, Texas.

P.J. recalls, "I remember going down with Dad and one by one he shut down the big Bessemers. All of a sudden it was deathly quiet. We walked back up to the house and all three of us sat at the kitchen table for a long time without talking. I'll never forget the silence. It seemed to intensify our sadness. We didn't want to leave."

The family gathered their personal belongings and left the peaceful community they loved. They left friends they had known for years and the Methodist Church where Mrs. Primm had played the organ.

The little boy grew into a man, and with the money he made from selling rivets, pursued a college degree. He still lives in Goliad, Texas but makes frequent trips to Wetumka, Oklahoma for class reunions and to visit friends who still live in the Phillips Plant area. P.J. says, "I did not want to move and leave my friends. The move had a profound effect on me. Oklahoma was my birthplace and I'm still drawn to where I grew up and the great life I lived at Phillips Plant."

Oliver Brinlee

AT the time P.J. and his family were leaving Phillips Plant, I. O. (Oliver) Brinlee was working from 10:00 p.m. until 6:00 a.m. at the ice plant in Wetumka. "I usually pulled thirty-five blocks of ice per shift. Each block weighed three hundred pounds. The blocks were pushed onto a chute where they were scored lengthwise by saws, and then tilted onto another chute and scored widthwise. The scored sections were then broken into fifty, twenty-five, and twelve and one-half pound blocks. These blocks were stored in the icehouse until they were sold for fifty cents, twenty-five cents, and fifteen cents," he explained.

Oliver was getting ready to go home one morning, when a neighbor came by to tell him he might get a job at Phillips Plant. Men were being transferred from Phillips Plant, because a new company had taken over. He went to apply for a job and was hired immediately.

"I didn't even get to go home and tell my wife," Oliver said. "Working at the plant was quite an experience. Plant production had been greatly reduced but there were still several engines running. Water was piped from a lake a mile north of the plant, and raw gas came from as far as Seminole and Okmulgee. That gas was processed into burnable products such as propane and gasoline.

"I kept on eye on things and made sure everything was operating like it was suppose to. One job was to switch the two big engines that powered the plant with electricity. Each engine alternated for twenty-four hours. The difficult part was getting the timing of the engine to be started in sync with the one that was running. If you messed up, all the electricity in the camp would go off. That made the boss very unhappy."

The Brinlee family moved to a farm near the plant and Mr. Brinlee farmed in addition to working for Phillips. After Phillips sold the plant to D-X Oil Company, he continued to work there. At the time it sold, only two engines were running. The plant closed in the early fifties.

"My last job there was disassembling engines and boxing up the usable parts to be shipped to Borger, Texas. Once all of the engines were torn down and the parts shipped I became a full time farmer."

Oliver and his wife, Madge, raised five children on their farm. Before bad health forced them to move to town, they were farming about 200 acres. Eighty acres were used for peanuts, the rest of the farm was planted in corn, cotton and soybeans. About 120 acres were used as pasture for cattle. When they moved to town, they took their house with them. Oliver's death in March of 2004 left Madge alone in the house that was once in a boomtown in Hughes County.

Phillips gasoline plant at Papoose City

Madge and Oliver Brinlee in 1938

Oliver Brinlee with his mule team ready to work the field

Brinlee family left to right: (standing) Curtis, Oliver,
Madge; (kneeling) Hartsell, Kenneth, Alton, and Pat

CHAPTER IV

The Purpose of the Oklahoma
Energy Resources Board (OERB)

The Founding

EIGHTY-EIGHT years have passed since Papoose City boomed. The community is sparsely populated with a few farms here and there. Most of the land is used for raising cattle or cutting hay.

The Papoose field is still producing a small amount of oil and natural gas. It has been estimated that from 1923 until the early fifties the 2, 200-acre oil field produced approximately twenty-seven million barrels of oil.

Many became rich when Papoose City was booming. Farmers leased their land for large amounts of money and were also paid part of the profits from production. Life was good for years. What had been overlooked was the damage being done to the land. Saltwater, which is produced along with oil, was not disposed of properly. In 1925, 22,085 barrels of saltwater were produced per day from 34 wells. This water was dumped into creeks or onto the ground. The result of such dumping is salt scars that deplete the soil and kill vegetation. Oil spills and saltwater became a concern to landowners so regulations were issued to control their disposal. These regulations greatly reduced further damage to the land but did nothing for the damage already done.

In 1992, the state legislator created the Oklahoma Energy Resources Board (OERB) to work with oil producers and royalty owners in restoring abandoned sites at no cost to the landowner. When a site has been submitted to the Oklahoma Corporation Commission it must be determined that there are no responsible parties to complete the restoration and therefore the site qualifies for restoration by the OERB. The OERB forwards the site to Beacon Environmental who in turn sends a field representative to the site and determines the extent of damage and necessary steps for restoration.

The Requirements for Reclamation

WHEN I became aware of the OERB I decided to investigate the process of getting our farm restored. First I contacted the Corporation Commission. A few days after my call a representative came to inspect the salt scars, (bare areas where vegetation would not grow), jagged ravines (formed from salt water running across the land), large concrete blocks (foundations for oil derricks) and sludge pits (shallow ponds that were build to hold the waste produced from drilling). After a tour of the farm, I was informed that BEACON Environmental would be notified. Beacon in turn would inspect the land to see if it qualified under OERB guidelines.

Greg Cook, projects manager with Beacon Environmental, called and made an appointment to survey the damaged areas on our farm. When the day arrived I rode shotgun with Greg and pointed out the salt scars, abandoned well sites, and concrete foundations that remained from long ago. All of the areas were flagged and photographed. Greg explained that his findings would be evaluated and if approved by OERB he would return and collect soil and water samples from the saltwater damaged areas. These samples would determine what amendments were necessary to return the soil to its natural state. In most cases the amendments are gypsum and organic matter.

Gypsum reduces the salt that is in the dirt that was once productive soil, and the organic matter is applied to allow the soluble salts to be flushed from the root zone.

The week after Greg took soil samples he called to tell me that there would be several trucks assembled at the flagged sites the next morning. He went on to explain that these were contractors looking over the work that needed to be done. Each contractor would turn in a bid on what they would charge to do the restoration. Once a contractor was selected work would begin.

Work began the following Monday. Bulldozers and other heavy equipment were hauled in to bury the large concrete foundations and other debris. Tractors and disks turned the soil after the dozers sloped and smoothed the rugged areas that resulted from saltwater runoff. Amendments were added to the newly tilled soil and grass was planted.

In the summer of 2001 the work was completed. The saltwater

creek that I played in as a child now has grass growing and erosion has been stopped. All of the concrete blocks that held oil derricks are gone. In a few years the land will be like it was eighty-eight years ago.

The Cost of Reclamation

ACCORDING to the OERB, of the 2,200 acres included in the Papoose field, 21 projects containing 126 sites have been completed at a cost of $476,000. Since 1994 more than 11,000 orphaned or abandoned sites in Oklahoma have been restored totaling a sum of 58 million. Of those projects 1,663 were located in Seminole County, 373 in Hughes County, and 424 were in Okfuskee County.

If you take a drive to where Papoose City once thrived, you will find no evidence that the town ever existed. You will see four tall stately smokestacks, all that remains of the Phillips Plant, overlooking a few pump jacks still bringing up black gold. And if you listen carefully, you may hear the sound of music and the laughter of a girl who loved to dance.

Remains of the Phillips Gasoline Plant

Smokestacks

Sentinel overlooking the remaining pumpjacks in the area
that once was the Papoose Field

Concrete foundation

Concrete foundations buried

Saltscars caused by saltwater running across low areas

Sloped land to prevent more soil erosion

Oil well site and saltwater damage

Amending the soil so grass can be planted

APPENDIX

"Philnews" monthly publication by Phillips Oil Company

Map of Hughes County showing location of
Papoose Field (see top left of center)

THE HOLDENVILLE DEMOCRAT
Holdenville, Okla., September 17, 1925

NEW PAPOOSE SCHOOL BUILDING BEING BUILT

Construction of a new school building at Papoose is under way and will be completed some time next week, according to Miss Alice Means, county superintendent of schools. The building will be a modern three room frame structure and will be the second school building in Papoose.

Vol. XXIX
No. 111
Page 5
Column 2

HOLDENVILLE DEMOCRAT
Holdenville, Okla. Thursday, Dec. 25, 1924

Waite Phillips to Build
Big plant at Wetumka

A large force of men are working with all possible haste on a 13 unit absorption gasoline plant near Wetumka for Waite Phillips. The investment will run around two million dollars, it is said, and is one of the largest of the kind in the United States. It will turn out 30,000 gallons of gasoline every day when in full operation. The Waite Phillips company has been very active in the development of the Hughes county field and has a number of producing wells from which it will ????? own product. Offices and warehouses as well as loading docks will be established at such points as will best serve the interest of the company.

Vol. 26
No. 18
Page 1
Column 1

News articles regarding Papoose Field

Block No. 6   Town Slick City

Our Number	R. P.	GRANTEE	G.O.	INST.	DATE of INST.	GRANTEE	FILED									
58 355		Slick City Town Co.		Deed	2 / 13 / 25		2 13 25								7	
44 22		A. J. Smith		Contr	3 / 1 / 25		3 20 25									
5086		Queens Robert to A. J. Smith			1 29 / 25		1									
		Queens Robert to A. A. Smith			Dec 5 18 25											
59 510		J. A. Arthur, Edgar Link			Feb 5 25 25		5 29 25									

Block 4 Slick City

492		Dist. Lew, Osage Ry, Rck to Lk Co ve W. W. Lonesome 2 23 25														6

1-12-10

Blocks leased at Slick City

Name of Parent (or Guardian): A. F. Mc Casland   Post Office: Papoose

Name of Township or Street: Yeager   Section or Street No.:

Name of Tribe: (If Indian or Freedman, give name of tribe.)

NAME OF CHILD	COLOR	SEX	DATE OF BIRTH			AGE	Deaf, Dumb, Blind, Feeble Minded and Crippled (Write Which)
			Month	Day	Year		
Ethel McCasland	W	F	July	12	1913	15	
Borjene	"	"	Aug.	13	1915	13	
Lois	"	"	July	18	1922	6	
Allen	"	m	Aug	13	1918	10	
Melvin	"	"	Sept.	13	1920	9	

I hereby declare under oath that the above is a true and correct statement of the facts given; that I am a legal resident of the above School District and the names and ages of all persons of school age are correct as written above.

A. F. McCasland, Parent or Guardian.

Subscribed and sworn to before me this the 8 day of Feb. , 1929.

T. O. Townsend, Enumerator.

Name of Parent (or Guardian): J. W. Ison   Post Office: Papoose

Name of Township or Street: Yeager   Section or Street No.:

Name of Tribe: (If Indian or Freedman, give name of tribe.)

NAME OF CHILD	COLOR	SEX	DATE OF BIRTH			AGE	Deaf, Dumb, Blind, Feeble Minded and Crippled
			Month	Day	Year		
Cloyd Ison	W	m	July	3	1921	4	

I hereby declare under oath that the above is a true and correct statement of the facts given; that I am a legal resident of the above School District and the names and ages of all persons of school age are correct as written above.

J. W. Ison, Parent or Guardian.

Subscribed and sworn to before me this the day of , 192.

T. O. Thomas, Enumerator.

Boswell v State
258 P. 1074
37 Okl.Cr. 429
Oklahoma Court of Criminal Appeals

Cite as: 1927 OK CR, 37 Okl.Cr.429,258 P. 1074

(Syllabus.)

Intoxicating Liquors –Conviction for Transporting not Sustained.

In a prosecution for transporting intoxicating liquor, evidence considered, and held insufficient to sustain a conviction.

Appeal from County Court, Hughes County: Owen H. Rives, Judge.

Fred Boswell was convicted of transporting intoxicating liquor, and he appeals. Reversed.

Huggins & Huser, for plaintiff in error.

Edwin Dabney, Atty. Gen., for the state.

Doyle, P.J. Appellant was convicted on a charge of unlawfully transporting one gallon of alcohol from the W.B. drug store in Slick City to another point in Hughes county, about-three-quarters of a mile east of Slick City, and in accordance with the verdict of the jury was sentenced to pay a fine of $100 and confinement in the county jail for 30 days.

Page 430

The errors assigned are, in substance, that the verdict is contrary to the law and the evidence: that the court erred in admitting evidence obtained by an illegal search and seizure; and that the court erred in excluding competent evidence offered by appellant.

The state relied for this conviction upon the testimony of L.C. Stockton, to the effect that he drove up to the appellant, who was driving east in a car from Slick City, and stopped him and asked him what he had in the car, and appellant said it was alcohol; that he found a gallon can of alcohol in the car; that he did not have a search warrant or warrant for the arrest of appellant. He was then asked if three-quarter of a mile east of Slick City was in Okfuskee county and failed to answer.

On redirect, he stated that the place he arrested appellant was not east of Slick City; that appellant was driving along the section line and most of the time his car was on the Hughes county line.

The testimony of this witness was admitted against the objections of appellant that the same was obtained by an illegal search and seizure.

At the close of the evidence for the state, counsel for appellant moved the court to instruct the jury to find him not guilty, on the further ground that the poor showed the offense, if any was committed in Okfuskee county, which motion was overruled.

Appellant testified that he was employed by the W.B. pharmacy in Slick City, now called Papoose; that the proprietor was a registered pharmacist. The county attorney objected to any testimony as to what appellant was doing "as having nothing to do with the case," which objection was sustained.

Counsel for appellant thereupon offered to show, if permitted to testify. "that he was employed by a regularly registered pharmacist conducting the W.B. pharmacy in the city of Papoose, Okfuskee county, that on this day said registered pharmacist also owned the W.B pharmacy No. 2 in Okfuskee county, and directed appellant, as his employee, to deliver this gallon of alcohol to W.B. pharmacy No. 2 for the purpose of using the same in his business according to the laws of the state of Oklahoma. "The court overruled the offer.

The testimony further shows that both or the W.B. Pharmacies, Nos. 1 and 2, are in Okfuskee county.

Sustaining the state's objection was error. However, we deem it sufficient to say that on the undisputed facts the testimony of the state's witness was illegally obtained and improperly received.

The judgement of the lower court is therefore reversed.

EDWARDS and DAVENPORT, JJ., concur.

Sources Consulted

The Oklahoma Energy Resource Board (3555 NW 58 Oklahoma City, Oklahoma 73112)

Greg Cook, Environmental Scientist (Wewoka, Oklahoma)

Phillip Landers of Landers and Musgrove Oil Producers (Okemah, Oklahoma)

Mattie Dillman (Wewoka, Oklahoma)

Gertie Reed (Sapulpa, Oklahoma)

Ethel Grace (Okemah Oklahoma)

Loise Chastain (Charleston, Arkansas)

Billy Bob Richardson (Shawnee, Oklahoma)

P.J. Primm (Goliad, Texas)

Oliver Brinlee (Holdenville, Oklahoma)

Oklahoma Geological Survey, Chas. N. Gould Director, Bulletin No. 36, Petroleum Engineering in the Papoose Oil Field

About the Author

Judy Goodspeed is a graduate of East Central State College in Oklahoma and was a Junior High School teacher and coach for thirty years.

She has been a contributing writer for *The Wewoka Times* and has written articles for *Outdoor Oklahoma*, *Good Old Days*, and *The Ketchpen*. Judy is a member of the Professional and Amateur Writers Society (PAWS) and of Oklahoma Writers Federation Inc. (OWFI).

She is the author of the non-fiction book Cowboy Sweethearts. She is also the author of several children's picture books, including: Perky Turkey Finds a Friend, Perky Turkey's 4th of July Adventure, Perky Turkey's Perfect Plan, and Saddle Up.

INDEX

Slick, Tom: 10, 34, *43*
Snomac, Oklahoma: 38
South Canadian River Bridge: 39
Spartan Aircraft: 41
St. Louis, Missouri: 40-41
Swain, Ma and Pa: 35
Snyder, Texas: 40

T ~
Tomlinson, Naomi: 7
Thompson's Store: 47-48

Tucumcari, New Mexico: 20

V ~
Vaughn, Lefty: 35

W ~
Wewoka, Oklahoma: 18-19, 21, 37-38, 74
Wingo, Johnnie: 7

* * *

www.ingramcontent.com/pod-product-compliance
Lightning Source LLC
Chambersburg PA
CBHW031608040426

42452CB00006B/444